KIDS MOVE!

BIBLE STORIES WITH EXERCISE
JESUS LIVES!

BY: KELLY WENNER

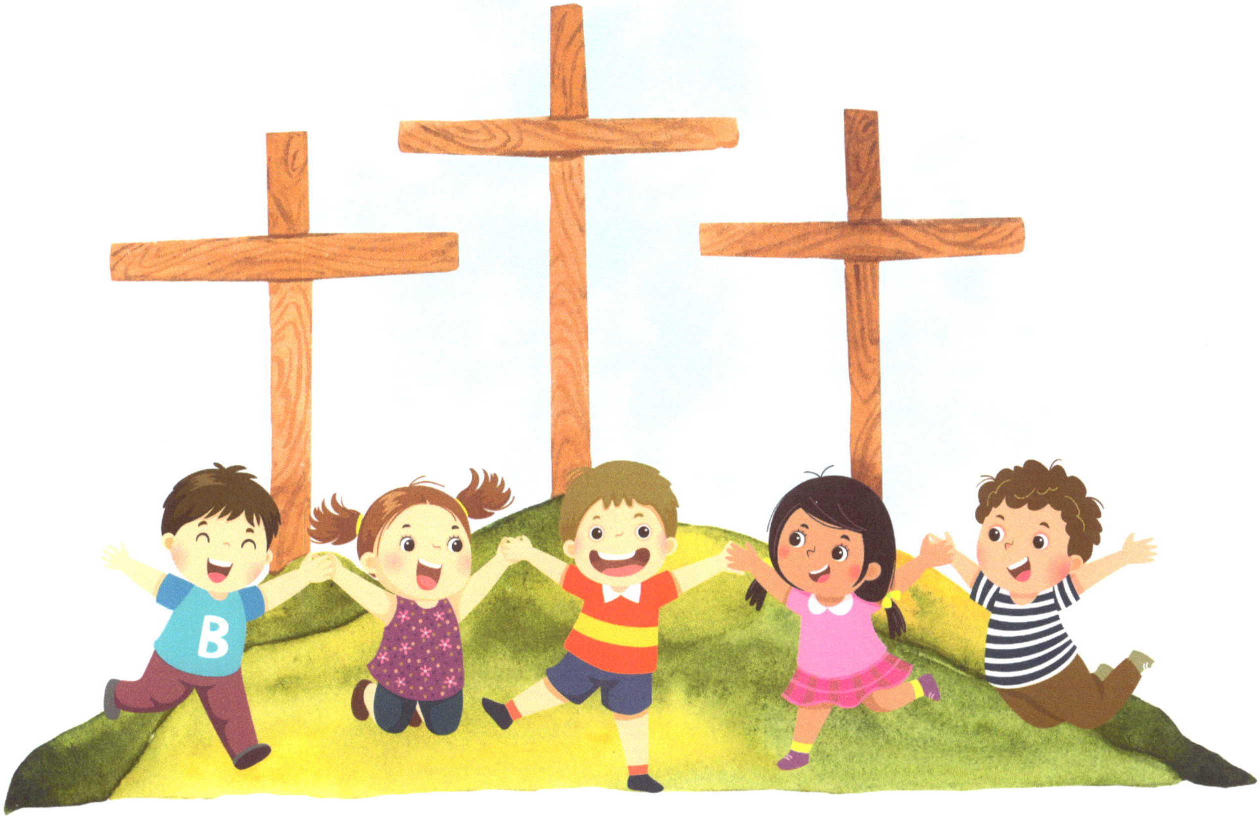

Kids Move!: Jesus Lives!
Written by Kelly Wenner

Copyright © 2025 by SoulStrength Fit
All rights reserved.
No part of this publication may be reproduced, distributed, or transmitted in any form or by any means, including photocopying, recording, or other electronic or mechanical methods, without the prior written permission of the publisher, except in the case of brief quotations embodied in critical reviews and certain other noncommercial uses permitted by copyright law.
For permission requests, contact:
SoulStrength Fit www.soulstrengthfit.com
ISBN: 979-8-9929143-2-0

This Book Belongs to:

_____

"HE IS NOT HERE, FOR HE HAS RISEN, JUST AS HE SAID!"

MATTHEW 28:6

Introduction

Welcome to Kids Move!: The True Story of Easter!
This book is part of the Kids Move! series—designed to help bring Bible stories to life with fun, interactive movement! Through simple actions and playful motions, children can experience God's Word in a way that's active, hands-on, and unforgettable.
As kids jump, stretch, and act out the story, they'll discover the incredible truth of Jesus' death and resurrection—all while staying engaged and having fun!

Hey, Kids!

Get ready to move!
This isn't just a story—it's an Easter adventure!
Every time you see the "Let's Move!" symbol, that's your chance to jump in and act out part of the story. You'll move, play, and celebrate the greatest story ever told—Jesus is alive!
So find a little space to move around, and let's begin the story of that first Easter morning.
Are you ready? Let's Move!

Long ago, our world experienced the saddest day ever.

It was the day Jesus was crucified on the cross.
Many people didn't understand that Jesus was the Son of God.
Because they didn't understand, they thought He should be punished. So, they handed Him over to be killed.

Something amazing happened when Jesus was crucified.
It was about lunchtime on what had been a bright, sunny day when they hung Jesus on the cross.

Let's Move!

Jump up and spread your arms wide like the shining sun! Jump high and show how bright the day is!

But just then, right as they hung Jesus on the cross, the sun stopped shining. Darkness covered the whole land, and it stayed dark for three whole hours while Jesus hung on the cross.

Let's Move!

Come up, and like the hands of a clock, let's spin in 3 circles to show three hours passing.
1… 2… 3!

Then, Jesus took His last breath.

At that very moment, the earth began to shake!
A powerful earthquake rumbled through the land.
The ground trembled, mountains shook, and great rocks split apart.
Stones rolled down hills as the whole earth quaked.

Let's Move!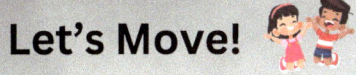

Jump side to side with big jumps, waving your arms over your head—the earth is shaking!
Now, jump over all the splitting, rolling stones!

In the middle of the earthquake, something incredible happened—
The giant curtain in the temple tore in two!

This wasn't just any curtain—it was huge, reaching high to the ceiling. It had separated people from God's holy presence.
But at the very moment Jesus took His last breath, the curtain ripped from top to bottom! Now, nothing could keep people from coming to God!

Let's Move!

Start jumping and reaching as high as you can—try to touch the top of the curtain!
Keep jumping from top to bottom, top to bottom—just like the curtain tore in half!

Many of the guards who had been standing under the cross trembled in fear.
With wide eyes, they exclaimed, "He really must have been the Son of God!"

Let's Move!

Tremble, tremble, tremble! Shake your hands and knees like you're shaking with fear!

Jesus' body was taken down from the cross, wrapped in clean linen, and placed in a tomb cut out of rock, like a cave.
A huge stone was rolled in front to seal it shut. No one could move it!

Let's Move!

Come up and try to push this giant rock!
Squat down low and push—squat and push!
It's so heavy—keep pushing and pushing!

The huge stone was finally in place, sealing the tomb and protecting Jesus' body.

His friends, followers, and all who loved Him left sadly, their hearts heavy with sorrow.

But this is not the end of the story!
In fact, this is where the best part begins!
It all started three days after Jesus' death.

Let's Move!

How many days? Three!
Let's do jumping jacks as we count!
1, 2, 3!

It was very early on the third day after Jesus' death. The sun was just beginning to rise, filling the sky with light.

One of Jesus' dearest friends, Mary, was walking with other women to visit His tomb.
It was a long road to get there.

Let's Move!

Come down to your hands and toes and make your body long and straight like the road to Jesus' tomb.

Now hop up and walk with the women—step, step, step.
Look! There it is just ahead!
Let's pick up the pace—run, run, run!

Just as the women approached the tomb, the ground suddenly shook—another earthquake!

Let's Move!

Jump side to side, wave your arms overhead, and shake like the earthquake is rumbling beneath your feet!

The women fell to the ground, terrified.

Let's Move!

Fall down to the ground like the women!

Mary looked up from where she had fallen, and she could not believe her eyes—the giant rock that had sealed the tomb was rolled away!

Afraid that someone had taken Jesus' body, Mary and her friends jumped up and rushed to the tomb.

Let's Move!

Hurry! Jump up and run, run, run to peek inside!

When the women stepped inside the tomb, they couldn't believe what they saw!

The white cloth that had covered Jesus' body was lying on the floor in a big heap—but Jesus was gone!

The women stared at the pile of cloth, bewildered and confused.

Suddenly, two men in clothes that gleamed like lightning stood beside them.
These weren't just ordinary men—they were angels!

Let's Move!

Jump and flash your arms like big bolts of lightning!
Now, float your arms gently like angel wings, just like the angels in the tomb.

Terrified, the women fell to their knees, bowing with their faces to the ground!

But the angels said, "Jesus is not here! He is not dead! He has risen—just as He said He would!"

This is the single most important moment in all of history!
This is the moment the whole world should rejoice!

Let's Move!

Jump and celebrate! Do a happy dance!
Rejoice with the angels in heaven and everyone on earth!
Jesus is alive! He's alive!

The women couldn't wait to tell all of Jesus' friends and family the amazing news!

Jesus had risen from the dead—just as He said He would!
They rushed back down the long road to get home.

Let's Move!

Run, run, run!

It was a long road home!

Now, come down to your hands and toes and make your body long and straight like the road back from the tomb!

Finally, Mary and her friends shared the incredible news with Jesus' closest friends!

After they found the empty tomb, Jesus appeared—first to Mary, then to His friends, and to many, many others!

He showed them His hands and feet, where the nails had pierced Him. He ate with them, comforted them, and taught them.

Jesus stayed with them for 40 days after He rose from the dead! How long? 40!

Let's Move!

Let's count by 10s with jumping jacks to get to 40!
10, 20, 30, 40!

At the end of 40 days, Jesus was taken up to Heaven in a big white cloud.

Let's Move!

Come down low, then rise up, up, up like the cloud lifting Jesus to Heaven!

Now, jump and reach as high as you can—keep jumping and reaching all the way into the sky!

Jesus' friends stared up into the sky as He disappeared.
But they weren't sad—they knew He had gone to Heaven to be with the Father. And they knew that one day, He will return to earth again!

Before Jesus went to Heaven, He gave His friends and followers a very important message.

Want to know what it was?

Jesus told His friends that He came to earth to save every person from their sins.

He died on the cross but rose from the dead so that anyone who believes in Him will live with Him forever in Heaven!

And do you know what?

Jesus wants YOU to share this good news with others too!

Let's Move!

Bring your hands to your heart and close your eyes.

Jesus, we are so happy that You rose from the dead so that we may live with You forever and ever in Heaven.

Amen!

JESUS IS ALIVE!
NOW GO SHARE THE GOOD NEWS!

About the Author

Kelly Wenner is the creator of SoulStrength Fit and SoulStrength Fit Kids, programs that bring together faith, fitness, and fun for both adults and children. With over 20 years of teaching experience and a master's degree in education, Kelly has a passion for making Bible stories come alive in creative and meaningful ways.

As a mom and educator, Kelly understands how important it is to help kids connect with God's Word in ways that are both memorable and active. That's why SoulStrength Fit Kids uses movement-based activities to turn Bible lessons into experiences kids will never forget.

Kelly lives in Southern California with her husband and three daughters. Her mission is to inspire families to grow in faith and live strong, joyful lives that glorify God.

✨ Want more fun, faith-filled learning?
Move to the video version of this story at SoulStrengthFitKids.com!

www.ingramcontent.com/pod-product-compliance
Lightning Source LLC
Chambersburg PA
CBHW060809090426
42736CB00003B/215